ROUTE
TO
SUCCESS

ROUTE TO SUCCESS

SUCCESS

An American Dream Tale

AHILE NICOLAS KOUDOU

CONTENTS

My Parents

This autobiography is dedicated

. . . to my deceased parents, Marceline Deh and Zaza Koudou, who gave me the opportunity and space to attend school and learn Western civilization, and the gift of vision. Their souls have showed me how to survive through life's hardships. From them, I learned determination, perseverance, optimism, power of drive, and the endless range of promises in life. Earlier in my life, my parents thought I was a gifted child, and if God willing, I was going to excel in all my endeavors. Until today, this credence has been the key for my success.

To my children—Pacome, Odio, Sika, Nadé, Nainon, and Ahilé Koudou Jr. I express my gratitude to them for their great love and extend my thanks to my spouse, Laurence Toilehi-Koudou, for her encouragement and endless love.

This autobiography materialized shares my lifetime experience and sends a message to the future generation that hard work, courage, determination, perseverance, and strong desire to succeed can always lead to fulfillment of better life and accomplishment. Many challenges, strains, and pain have often left me physically and emotionally exhausted as I have gone through my academic and/or professional life. However, my self-confidence, self-esteem, pride, values, commitment to edification, and devotion to hard work are the major forces that helped me successfully reach my goals and be able today to share my legacy of success in this manuscript.

CHAPTER 1

Building a Foundation for Success

CÔTE D'IVOIRE IS a country located in the western corner of the African continent between Liberia in the west and Ghana in the east. Mali and Burkina Faso share their borders with Côte d'Ivoire in the north and the Gulf of Guinea in the south. Côte d'Ivoire is the largest producer of cocoa beans, with 40 percent of the world market, and the fifth producer of coffee in the world. I was born a few years before its independence, on August 7, 1960. For more than three decades, the country enjoyed the economic growth and political stability, under the sole leadership of Félix Houphouët-Boigny, the father of the nation.

My parents, who were small farmers of cocoa and coffee, thought that the future of the new generation of citizens of the Côte d'Ivoire lay in their education. Well-educated children could replace the colonial masters to lead the destiny of their newly independent country. My parents, who needed labor force to assist them in their daily farming tasks, decided to send me to school. There were no schools in my community because under the colonial rules, the only schools could be found in large cities and our most populated rural areas. My native village, Doukouyo, did not conform to the norms to have a regional primary school.

All children born in this community had to leave their parents, friends, and siblings if they were chosen to receive formal education. The nearest school was six miles from Doukouyo. No road access was available. The only way to travel from my native community to Balouepalegnoa, where the regional school was located, was to walk and cross creeks and ponds through the jungle. It was a painful decision for the parents and a difficult decision as well for us elected children to attend French formal school. At first, I did not welcome the idea of being away from my parents so young and could not understand how important my parents' decision was to impact my adult life. My nights were long and days sad. Despite all the risks, my parents did not give up their dream for me to attend French school. My khaki uniform and plastic shoes were bought. My mom was thirty-five years younger than my father; together they had six children, including myself. As a blended family, we were thirty children in total. All our half brothers and sisters were far older than us. I am the second child of my mother. My older sister and I were partners in the decision to attend formal French school. We were very lucky to be chosen for that purpose among many other children.

When it was time for us to leave our village to attend the school in Balouepalegnoa for the first time, one of the oldest boys of the family, Big Brother Maurice Gnahore, went with us to assist in registration for school and find a place where we could stay. The plan was that my older sister Agnes and I could not live in the same family because we had to learn the survival skills and gain maturity. Thus, Agnes and I had different host families. Suddenly, my environment was different, and the attention that my parents were giving me was gone. I felt alone and had to learn the survival skills. Every morning I had to get up very early to go get fresh water in the creek outside the village. I was scared to death because of the presence of some dangerous snakes one could meet on the trail leading to the creek. But I did not have a choice; I had to mature prematurely and be responsible for myself. This exercise of carrying the water can on my head to bring it home and take a cold bath was tedious and tiring. Often I was many hours late to school with an empty stomach. Mr. Boni Alfred, who was the school principal and my first-grade teacher, had faith in me. He knew I was an intelligent child, and with a little care and attention, I could excel. He was doing his best every day during lunchtime to take me home and feed me. I managed to continue my school mission and remain in the host family as well, despite the hostile environment. After the first school year ended and my sister and I returned to Doukouyo, my native village, I told my parents that I did not want to go back to my host village to pursue the dream to acquire my schooling foundation.

My parents, who felt that I had a rebellious attitude toward school, spoke to me. "Son, do you really think sending you away to get educated is planned strategy to keep you away from home? No, but it is because we love you so much, we are forced to send you away to attend school. For twenty years from now, the kind of life that my spouse and I are living might be obsolete. So if I do not send you to school, I would have made a serious mistake and would have denied opportunities to an entire generation, namely my grandchildren." Until today, this thought has been the strength for my success. All along my schooling, my parents' strong commitment and inspiring words remained my strength and a big source of motivation for my success. The route has been long and painful somehow and rewarding at the end.

In Côte d'Ivoire, to access middle school just after six years of elementary school, there is a national exam where only the best students in the country would be selected. The few top students will have the opportunity to go to the next level. Since none of my parents were formerly educated in French school, I could not get help while away and even when I was at home. I was eleven years old when I first competed for the exam. I was given another opportunity to retake the same national exam the following year. Once again, I failed it, but I succeeded in obtaining my primary school certificate, just a diploma. I had one more chance to take the middle school entrance exam, and this time, it was good. I brilliantly completed the middle school with the Brevet d'Etude du Premier Cycle (BEPC) after four academic years, and passed the entrance exam to high school. I could already dream about a rich professional career because I had faith in my success. After three years of hard work in high school, I obtained my high school certificate called baccalaureate. I was seen by my peers, parents, and friends as a hardworking student with a bright future ahead. College- bound students were highly respected. The government of Côte d'Ivoire had dorms and cafeterias in the major districts of Abidjan, the economic capital of the country. We as students had our own buses to take us to and from the campus. Each student had a stipend of an equivalent of a hundred dollars per month, and the transportation was free. Room and board were about twelve dollars per month as well. Life as a young man was enjoyable, and I could already see myself as a political elite. My concentration was in history/geography.

High School student at Lycee De Dimbokro, Cote d'Ivoire-
Year I successfully completed my High School diploma

We did not have any choice as to what our concentrations were as the government decided our field of specialization. My dream was to become the first lawyer in my family and community; lawyers had a respectable reputation and a bright future for the newly independent country. In the meanwhile, my older sister got married and started her family. I was the only one left to go on to higher education, the hope of my immediate family and the entire community as well. I was the first young man to have succeeded so far as to receive a university education. My first year in college was traumatic and not fruitful because I realized that I was failing. The only way to improve the social status was through education. However, I had the opportunity to retake the freshman year. During my second year, I was still enrolled as freshman at L'Ecole Normale Supérieure d'Abidjan (ENS). I was involved in politics on campus for the candidacy of president of the student union, section of ENS, but I was disqualified because I was repeating my freshman year. In fact, nowhere in the status of the student union was there any statement disqualifying me, but the policy was tailored that year specifically to take care of my issue. In other words, the director of the ENS saw that I was an outspoken student activist and did not want such a person to be a student leader in his institution. The country of Côte d'Ivoire was under one party's rule, and no one was allowed to challenge the authority of Houphouët-Boigny. The director of ENS did not want to be seen as someone who was endorsing my views. The best thing for the school's authority was to dismiss me from the institution by any means, so with that, I again failed freshman year. All my grades were posted on the board, as well as those of other students on the campus.

Summer 1980- After my first year of college in Ecole Normale Superieure d'Abidjan, I was vacationing in Doukouyo in my native village with family members

No one was allowed to see the exam sheets to dispute the recorded grades or acknowledge our errors in the exams. There was no appeal process. Consequently, at the end of my second year of being a freshman, I was dismissed from the program. Some of my peers were also terminated, and some committed suicide. My friend Lamoussa Djinko and I had a strong commitment for our future. My philosophy about this unfortunate situation instilled in me a resolve to chart my own destiny. No one was going to decide my future. I said to myself, "The route to success will be long, but at the end, I will prevail, just wait and see." At this moment, I assessed my life all night to see what I have done wrong to be in this position and what I could do to turn this failure into a success. My first thought was to leave Côte d'Ivoire and to travel abroad to pursue my studies. During that period, I met another friend named Kesse Bongroh on the campus of Yopougon. We shared our experiences, and it happened that we had the same ambition. He had the mastery of the French language and was very convincing. The ideas to pursue our studies overseas were abundant, but resources were lacking to keep up with our ambitions. As a quick solution to our educational objective, my friend wanted us to go to the Soviet Union, where, for him, our educational goals could be endorsed by the Soviet government. I did not endorse his idea because I was rejecting communism and the Russian language was not widely spoken. Upon our return to Côte d'Ivoire, I did not want to have some ideological problems. At this moment, I came up with a list of things that I could do honestly to fulfill my dream. One of the ideas was to sign up to go to teacher training school and, after one academic year of training, to become a teacher of an elementary school and make some income to fulfill my ambition. My friend Kesse concurred, and we submitted our paperwork to enter a teacher training school called CAFOP Supérieur. My other friend Lamoussa Djinko remained in Abidjan and was preparing to leave the country for the same objective. Lamoussa's parents had some financial resources to send their son abroad immediately. Lamoussa chose the United States of America to pursue his studies and promised that he would never leave me in Côte d'Ivoire. It was in 1981 that we planned the strategies of our lives. That same year, Lamoussa realized his goal to study abroad and traveled to the USA. Kesse and I were admitted to teacher training school. Kesse went to Bouake, the second largest city of Côte d'Ivoire, and I remained in Yamoussoukro, the capital and administrative city. Living apart, three of us had the same conviction, which was to leave the country. Even our love lives could not override the strong dedication to pursue our education away from home.

While in teacher training school, I became the leader of future teachers. There, two groups were in rivalry. The newly graduated students from high school who did not have the opportunity to pursue their higher education were given the opportunity to become elementary school teachers against their will, and people like me who did not fulfill their dream to graduate from university voluntarily applied to be a teacher. Being a leader of these two groups was very challenging, and I was not sure what I was getting into. The freshly graduated students from high school wanted a presalary from the government if they had to become elementary school teachers. The second group, the former college students who chose to become teachers, was docile. The differences among these two groups brought tension on campus. As a leader, I had to face these challenges. I wasted no time in starting a negotiation with the government of Côte d'Ivoire to secure a deal between the government and the future teachers' union. The presalary request was on the agenda in all teacher training schools nationwide. I used my charisma to invite the representatives of each teacher training school to meet in Yamoussoukro in fall of 1981 to come up with a common agenda to address our claim. During that meeting, I was chosen as a national representative of the student teachers' union. A national committee was formed. Immediately, we started the negotiation with the government, with the main objective to secure a presalary for student teachers. Unfortunately, the result of the negotiation was unsatisfactory. I must say that Yamoussoukro is the hometown of the father of the nation, Felix Houphouët-Boigny. In Yamoussoukro, teachers in training school started to protest the unpopular decision of the government to refuse to pay the presalary of student teachers. The campus of Yamoussoukro was closed; the students responsible for the revolt were terminated, and again some of them committed suicide because they lost hope in a country where the unemployment rate was in two digits. Since I was strongly opposed to the students' revolt, I resigned my position as leader and managed to survive. My main objective was to complete my training and secure an employment to reach my goals to study abroad. At that end, I took everything seriously and finalized my training. The diploma of Instituteur Stagiaire was granted. My first teaching position was in the village of Gbetitapea, where I would have taught third-grade children.

1981-Member of Soccer team in teachers training School in Yamoussoukro, Cote d'Ivoire

CHAPTER 2

Brief Transition

IN JUNE 1982, I completed my teacher training and was preparing for my new position. *Teacher*, in this manuscript, only refers to someone who is teaching in elementary schools. Thus, with the influx of newly trained teachers, the government of Côte d'Ivoire was able to meet the goal of staffing schools nationwide. The academic year 1982–1983 was on schedule to start on September, and teachers already knew to which school they will be assigned as early as July.

As a result, they had enough time for them to get ready and go to their assigned schools to meet with their pupils, parents, and the community, and adjust to their new environment. I was so excited about this new opportunity because my dream to leave Côte d'Ivoire and go to America to pursue my education was about to be realized. I knew that after working for ten months, I would receive my back payment, which would substantiate the income needed to realize my dream of traveling abroad to pursue my studies. Hence, the government of Côte d'Ivoire asked to join the elementary school of Gbetitapea, located three hundred kilometers from Abidjan, the administrative and banking city of the nation. It is also the largest city of Côte d'Ivoire with more than four million inhabitants.

1982-My first month in Gbetitapea Village where I will serve a 3rd grade teacher

1982-1983 School year with my 3rd grade students at Gbetitapea. Year I left Cote d'Ivoire to come to USA to pursue my higher education

While in Gbetitapea, despite some distractions as a young man, my goal to travel abroad to pursue my education was always maintained. No other thing on earth could make me change my mind, but I was always devoted to my teaching profession. I loved my pupils, and for them, I was a good role model. Outside my teaching, I was their mentor, a counselor, and a role model for them. I did my best so that I could leave them a legacy and/or a great memory. I performed my job without showing that it was going to be short. Every night I had a heavy mental exercise about my dream. I would ask myself several questions. Will I keep my goal and drive to pursue my studies in the United States of America? And if I do not succeed, what will be my future and the one of my family? During my ten months tenure in Gbetitapea, I had lots of things to think about. There was no room to be bored. I was always praying that the government of Côte d'Ivoire would give me the ten months' pay. My wishes became a reality when in early June of 1983, I received a check of $4,500—a back pay as a remuneration of task performed. With such amount in my bank account, I knew that God had answered my devotions. I kept my travel plan a secret from my peers and even some of my siblings. My mother, who did not want me to leave my ailing father, was sturdily opposed to my plan. I had to talk to her seriously about my goals and how these goals were going to affect her grandchildren in the future and even her existence as a mother of six children. I told her that my success was going to be her own legacy as a caring mother. Finally, she realized that nothing was going to make me change my ambition and goal. At the end, she gave me her blessing, and I was released. Then I went to my older sister Mme. Agnes Affi to ask for assistance to get my passport and write me an affidavit of support to request my student visa. It was something she did not hesitate to do, and the visa was granted to me to leave Côte d'Ivoire for the United States. I left my native country for USA on July 15, 1983. I was very happy, but I also had mixed feelings because I was leaving my land of birth with all my childhood friends and was not sure when I was going to return. This was the only moment I seriously thought about my mother's concerns of me leaving them, but I quickly convinced myself that the decision of leaving everybody behind was wise and well-thought-out. At that particular moment, I decided to focus on my journey.

Thus, during my trip to New York, I met a very nice lady in the flight. She was in her sixties and was open-minded to assist me. This was my first international flight, and I needed assistance anyway. Her name was Ms. Kay Andrew, a retired high school teacher and a resident of New Jersey. She visited Africa and was on her way back to New York. We were sharing our seats during the journey. She asked me what the objective of my trip to America was, because she thought I was visiting siblings in New York since it was in summer. I responded that I was going to the United States to pursue my dream of getting a college education. Then I added that my short-term objective was to learn the English language and later on be able to materialize my lifetime dream of being educated in such great country as the United States of America. This way, I could secure my professional career anywhere on the planet. Along with my native French language skills, the American education was going to open the door for me. And I planned to return to Côte d'Ivoire after the completion of my studies to contribute effectively to the development of my country of origin. This way, I will have a competitive advantage over the French-educated Ivorians in my professional career. This does not undermine the education of the Ivorian scholars trained in France, but I would have the slight competitive advantage of the

English language to secure a better position in the government. I also told her, "Until I left Côte d'Ivoire, I was just a teacher like you. But with this trip, I put an end to that profession," and she understood that we had something in common. She realized that I was a very dedicated young man who could be helped. She offered me her service upon our arrival to New York because it is a challenging city. Mrs. Andrew's love for humans and, most of all her willingness to assist me in New York built my confidence and strengthened my ambitious agenda to excel in America. Yes, the United States, a land of opportunity, was ready to welcome me. As long as I was going to be focused on my lifetime dream to succeed, I had full confidence that the future in America was promising. Even though my level of motivation was very high, I was still afraid about the challenges of living in America, but I had faith in God that I was going to prevail. Until today, I extend my gratitude to Mrs. Andrew for everything she has done to give me a short transition in America.

Chapter 3

Cultural Transformation and Determination to Acquire Higher Education

THE AIR AFRIQUE plane from Côte d'Ivoire landed in New York around 6:30 a.m. local time. The airport was tremendous for me, and everybody was in a hurry, going in different directions. It was the very first time I was a minority in a country where the majority of the population was Caucasian. This was the very first interesting experience in America. From that very day, I recognized that America was a fast-paced society, corresponding to the anecdote "Time is money." Most of the people I could see were in jeans, and everybody was speaking too fast for me. When I saw New York City, it was a very gigantic city. I did not know what to do to secure a hotel room in Manhattan. Ms. Kay Andrew, who knew this was my very first journey in America, came close to me and said slowly, "Do you need help? My friend will be here shortly, and we will be willing to find you a place. In fact, YMCA in Manhattan will be a perfect place for you to stay because it will be affordable for you." I did not waste my time and endorsed her idea to assist me.

A few minutes later, Ms. Kay Andrew's friend came to pick her up from JFK Airport, and we left for Manhattan. I was afraid of the ride because I was not really familiar with Ms. Andrew and her friend, but I was also confident that they were willingly helping me from the bottom of their hearts. Without the assistance of the couple, I was not sure where to go in New York City and where I could spend a couple of nights and be able to conduct my financial transaction. We landed in New York City from Africa on Saturday morning, and on Monday morning, I was scheduled to fly out of the city for Indianapolis, my final destination.

Hence, we left JFK Airport for Manhattan (downtown New York City), where I secured a room with YMCA. My English language skills were so limited, and being a minority African was even more intimidating. Upon my arrival in the YMCA, I managed to take a couple of hours' nap—something I needed to get for a full rest. Then I went out looking for a restaurant. I did not want to go too far because I was afraid of being lost and being in a situation where I would have to speak the very little English I know and be able to explain my situation for assistance. Luckily, a KFC restaurant was nearby. I decided to purchase my dinner there, but I did not know what to choose from the menu because KFC was my very first experience. One of the employees was nice enough to assist me. I bought an eight-piece bucket meal and started eating. I was expecting to have some rice, but mashed potato was served. I ate my meal with great appetite and satisfaction. This was the first time in my life I ate mashed potato. I enjoyed the KFC restaurant during my stay in New York until I left for Indianapolis.

Until then my friend Lamoussa Djinko, who was my host family, did not know I was on my way to Indianapolis to join him.

I thought this was going to be a great surprise for him. I landed in Indianapolis on July 18 at 2:00 p.m. Since I was not fluent in English, I wrote Djinko's address on an envelope and gave it to the taxi driver. He told me, "I know where it is." I responded to him, "Thank you." Twenty minutes later, the taxi driver dropped me at the exact address. Fortunately, Djinko was home and very happy to see me. After eating the lunch he cooked for the occasion, he called Frantz Victor, who came to meet with me as well. Frantz Victor, who was born in Haiti, speaks the French language just like Djinko and I. It did not take time for us to establish a neat relationship. Next day we went out for sightseeing, and upon our arrival in downtown Indianapolis, I felt the need to urinate. Like back home, I chose to do it on an empty and clean space. Both of my friends were surprised by the gesture and told me nicely, "Here in America, it is not appropriate to urinate outside on the edges of the streets and even while driving on the highway. Restrooms are provided to be used. You must quickly learn from your mistake." It was an advice I took seriously as I was very eager to learn and comply with the American tradition and culture. This was the very first most important cultural clang, and I realized I had to learn the culture quickly in my newly adopted country if I wanted to get along with many people.

I could also see that the American culture is open, rule-oriented, very individualized, detail-oriented in communication, proactive, and productive. This was a huge challenge to overcome if I wanted to reach my goals of being a successful immigrant in my newly adopted country. The new culture was more aptly applied to a specific environment, such as work or school, compared to the culture of my home country, Côte d'Ivoire. In addition to the different culture aspects you are required to learn and adapt to, the environment is also playing an important role. The cool and hot weather already had an effect on my dressing culture. I had to adapt to the winter clothes. Winter was not something I liked, but I had to be able to adjust to it. Summer was also horribly hot. It did not take time for me to know that living in North America was inspiring, and to succeed in such environment, one must be courageous and willing to adjust to the aforementioned challenges. Despite all these unfortunate situations of culture, tradition, and environment, I had one goal: to be able to get professional training that requires a formal higher education. But how can one meet that goal if the financial resources are limited or even inexistent? The only hope was a strong drive and creativity to overcome all challenges found on the road to success.

CHAPTER 4

Drive to Pursue
Higher Education in the USA

URSUING MY STUDIES in America was a lifetime dream for me. From my own experience, you do not need to come from a rich family to be educated, but you must have the drive, dedication, and high level of motivation to reach your goals. I arrived in America with $2,000 in my pocket. My main objective was to earn my college education, but I did not have any ideas how I could supplement my financial resources and I had no clear plan to materialize my objective. America has been known for many years as home of the capitalist ideology. Before my arrival in the United States, my friend Djinko, who had already spent more than twelve months in the United States, warned me about how money was more important than human relationships in the country of Uncle Sam. He said, "Don't ever show to your friends that you are lacking financial resources. If you do, you will be alone because no one would want to support your financial burden." As a good listener, I took his advice seriously before I left Côte d'Ivoire for a long journey in America. I knew I was in very serious financial trouble, and I did not have a choice other than to find short- and long-term solutions. As a short-term solution, I remember taking out a piece of paper to make the inventory of headers, such as the following: What are my strengths that I may be able to use to survive? What challenges do I face? What can I do to help myself get into school and succeed? I knew also that I had a fine personality and very good manner to meet a nice lady partner to share my cultural transformation with me. This thought was a long-term goal rather than a short-term strategy. I soon learned that my header's inventory was a technique used by top business executives embarking on existing businesses or new ventures. I had no idea I was conducting a SWOT analysis or that one day I would teach it to my students.

A SWOT analysis assesses the strengths, weaknesses, opportunities, and threats in decision-making. It was a personal SWOT analysis that helped me pursue and achieve my highest level of education. As strength, I could speak French, which is the national language in my country of origin. In the United States, it is a competitive advantage for me somehow. The French language skills became a money-earning tool. Then I made myself available to the American tourists willing to visit French-speaking African countries. In my neighborhood, I was tutoring middle and high school students in exchange to get paid. The cash money received was used to go on Indiana University–Purdue University Indianapolis (IUPUI) to attend classes that I did not register for. Sometimes I was attending classes with a large size, where the attendance could not be taken, to listen and learn how to take notes when the professors were lecturing for their classes. I was using these tactics to learn the college culture in America before having the necessary financial mean to pay my tuition and enroll in the academic program of my choice. For more than twelve months, I was not on any roster at IUPUI, but I was attending classes illegally. This unethical way of learning, which I will not advise people reading my memoir to do, would pay off in my life at the end.

On December 17, 1983, a friend of mine, David Kegan, a native of Kenya, organized a party to celebrate the completion of his bachelor's degree program in business. Djinko and I were invited to attend the party. After hesitating, we finally decided to be in attendance. It was a cold evening of December. One hour after our arrival, I saw a couple, a beautiful lady dressed in African attire and a tall, slim man, making their appearance in the room. I was not sure if the lady that I saw was in company with her husband or just a friend. My mind was busy observing her to find an opportunity to ask her to dance with me. Effectively, I was blessed to have that favor from the Lord. When I asked her to dance with me, she did not hesitate. It was during the dance on the floor that I introduced myself, and she did the same by giving me her name, N'Danu. At the end of the party, we exchanged our phone numbers, and since that night, our acquaintance became a romantic relationship. We were expecting a child then when we decided to strengthen our relationship. On March 20, 1984, N'Danu and I got married. I was inspired, very confident, and comfortable with my new spouse. She also loves the African culture and tradition. Even though she was born in America, she had enormous knowledge and an appreciation of African culture and tradition. From our union, Sika Bassou and Nadé SD were born. When N'Danu and I were wife and husband, most of the time, she was on my side while I was studying. She taught me how to write the proper English and speak the language. Everything moved smoothly for us because we were both very happy. The next step was to decide which institutions to select to continue my education. State institutions were affordable with in-state tuition benefits but too crowded to get the individual attention that I always wanted to have. Finally, I chose to attend private universities where the class sizes were manageable for me. As a result, I selected University of Indianapolis for my undergraduate degree work and Butler University for my master's in business administration degree work as well. After the aforementioned degree works, I felt confident to attend the state-founded institutions for the completion of my PhD degree. Louisiana State University was my choice. I am more than happy to acknowledge proudly in this manuscript that N'Danu has played an important role not only in my educational success but also in the successful competition of the doctorate degree of our daughter Sika Bassou Koudou. She deserves all my appreciation.

CHAPTER 5

Inspirational Career

UPON MY ARRIVAL in United States of America, I did not waste time to realize that the business culture in my newly adopted country was completely different from my country of birth, Côte d'Ivoire. The working days of the week were similar, but the hours were different. While in Côte d'Ivoire, the business culture tolerates longer hours of break from noon to 3:00 p.m., in America, thirty minutes are allowed for eight hours of work. The productivity at work is a norm if you want to succeed professionally in North America; while I was still going through the cultural adjustment and as a student, I quickly learned the American business culture. I understood that any deadlines related to work were the ultimate priority for an employee or staff. Anyone can complete a job, but the most important thing is how long a given work will take to be done. Completing the assigned work in a timely manner is the synonym of a job well done.

On top of the strong belief in high level of productivity, the average vacation time in United States is fourteen days, while thirty days are given as vacation time in Côte d'Ivoire. Facing this new working cultural environment, it was necessary to think and make a choice for my future profession. Hence, becoming a successful university professor was always my lifetime dream, and the working environment and culture on campus could fit my professional philosophy well. I knew already that the English language that I learned as an adult was a challenge, and being a professor, my efforts of learning English continuously were going to be very effective. I am a great achiever, and this way, I could continue not only to improve but also be able to educate students from different backgrounds to change their lives positively. I have always been very conscious about this responsibility of educating students. Thus, as an undergraduate student, I offered to be a teaching assistant in French language lab at the University of Indianapolis. I performed that duty with a great passion. Following are some of my students' autographs:

> To Koudou, with sincere appreciation and best wishes for your success. (French 101 by Lisa, Ken, Vickie Michelle, Jeff, Katie, Dan, and Jill, 1987)

> Your friendship has meant a lot to me. I'm happy to have met you in a class which I wasn't too enthused about taking. Everything worked out for the best (praise God). I'm so enthused about graduating. It won't be long now! Please keep in touch! (Jill Cooper)

> You have been a *Super* teacher and I've enjoyed having you in drill, I'm looking very forward to the day I get a card from you. I wish you good luck always. Take care and God bless. (Elaine Almeida)

1985 teaching Assistant at University of Indianapolis, Indiana, with French major students

Thus, the aforementioned observations and the students' remarks gave me the energy to definitively become a college professor. The other thing I had to do was talk to Dr. James Conrad, then senior professor of economics; Robin Livesay, former dean of the School of Business at University of Indianapolis; and Dr. Kwadwo Anokwa, retired professor and dean of the School of Journalism at Butler University. The aforementioned three educators were my most trusted individuals, advisors, and mentors. They were also my role models in the profession. Their input in my career choice was very meaningful to me. Dr. Anokwa was a unique mentor and inspirational one. He was one of the advisors who initiated me with academic conference presentation. In this regard, he coached me to present my first research paper at University of Michigan–East Lansing. After that day, I was mentally prepared to start my career. In summer of 1991, after I successfully completed my master's degree in business administration from Butler University (1989), I enrolled briefly in the PhD program in international economics at University of Denver– Colorado. Upon my return in Indianapolis in summer of 1992, I was hired as an instructor of marketing and/ or international business at the University of Indianapolis. This opportunity was my first teaching job as a college instructor. I knew that Dr. Conrad and Dr. Livesay fully trusted me to teach for them. This was a great responsibility, and I did not want to delude them. I had to demonstrate that my mentors' decision of making me an instructor of marketing and/or international business was not an illusion but rather a reality. Since then I realized that to be successful in any profession, one must love the job. Teaching is an obsession for me, and I was mentally prepared. As a consequence, and with great support of Dr. Anokwa, I went back to school to get a terminal degree.

This time my choice was in Louisiana State University, where all the costs of my studies were fully taken care. Dr. Richard Vlosky played an important role in my PhD work by inspiring me to do high-quality research work. He was very devoted to preparing me to be an excellent scholar. From him, I learned how to be focused and produce a well- thought and stimulating research work. I see him as someone who has had a great impact on my scholarly work among many others.

Upon the completion of my PhD degree program, I was hired at Park University as a part-time assistant professor on August 1998. One month after my appointment, the director of the MBA program resigned from her position, and I was asked to take over the leadership of the graduate program in business administration. I held that position for fourteen years before resigning to be just a senior professor of business administration. As an academic administrator and professor, I became a two-time J. William Fulbright Award scholar (2003 and 2009), thus I revamped the MBA curriculum to better fit the need of the employers, exponentially grew Park's master of business administration program, and contributed actively to the professional accreditation of Park University's MBA and school of business programs.

Today I take every opportunity to share my hard-earned wisdom with students by telling them that they must value their education. You must do it with pride, gratitude, and confidence. Despite the challenges you face, focus on your strengths to create the opportunities to achieve your dreams. If I can make it, you can too, with some efforts.

1998 graduated from the PhD Program at Louisiana State University

As a professor and Fulbright scholar, I taught and attended conferences around the world. Thus, I had firsthand teaching and research experiences in the Republic of Benin at Université of Calavy Cotonou, Benin, and Ghana Institute of Management and Public Affairs (GIMPA) in Accra, Ghana, respectively. I attended national and international conferences to disseminate my research on topics such as Freshwater Resource Management and Sustainable Economic Development, Impact of Culture in Small Business Enterprise Innovation in Africa and Effect of Arable Land Acquisitions and Dilemma of Sustainable Natural Resources Management in Sub-Saharan Africa, etc. All the aforementioned efforts became the legacy of a career that will be remembered by my children and grandchildren and those who will enjoy reading my autobiography.

ADDITIONAL PHOTOS...

*2012 Director of MBA Program at Park University Posing
for the School Magazine*

with my Mother

1999 Commencement Ceremony at Park University

1990 as an Adjunct French Faculty, I visited Doukouyo with a group of students from Butler University. This was a study tour in Cote d'Ivoire

ABOUT THE AUTHOR

Dr. Nicolas A. Koudou is a retired Professor of Business Administration and Director of Graduate Programs in Business Administration at Park University School of Business. Dr. Koudou was a two-time recipient of J. William Fulbright U.S. Scholar and the U.S. Department of State Scholar. He previously held Adjunct faculty positions at Butler University and the University of Indianapolis, Indiana; worked as visiting professor at "Université Africaine de Technologie et de Management, Institut Universitaire du Benin" in Republic of Benin and at Ghana Institute of Management and Public Administration (GIMPA) in Accra, Ghana. He also worked for several years as Associate Editor of African Journal of Business Management.

Dr. Koudou's second book **"Business Environment in Sub-Saharan Africa"** was released in 2019 and his research papers are published in a number of academic and professional journals such as the European Journal of Business and Management; the European Journal of Economics and Sustainable Development; the Journal of Management &World Business Research; the

International Journal of Business and Economic Perspectives; the International Journal of Business and Public Administration; the Forest Product Journal; the Ghana Journal of Forestry, and the African Development Bank Magazine. His research interests are in the area of Freshwater and Sustainable Economic Development; the Impact of culture in Small Business Enterprise Innovation in Africa; Prestige Marketing; Green Marketing; Hermetic marketing; Land Acquisitions and sustainable Natural Resources Management; Foreign Direct Investment; Sustainable Economic development; Forest Resources and Eco-tourism based Sustainable development; and International Trade and Marketing of Forest Products.

Professor Koudou's other academic recognitions include Park University President's Award for Teaching Excellence; Outstanding Park School of Business Faculty Award; MBA Distinguished Professor Award; three times winner of Who's Who Among America's Teachers and Member of Louisiana State University Chapter of the Honor Society of Agriculture, Gamma Sigma Delta.

Professor Koudou has taught Global Executive MBA seminars and courses and worked as a consultant in an online Curriculum Development and Redevelopment programs as well as Blended courses. As a consultant, Dr. Koudou evaluated Graduate Business Programs to ensure quality and effective curricula delivery. Dr. Koudou is the founder of the American University of Cote d'Ivoire in 2018.